MANTRA OF THE OPPRESSED

Mujeeb Jaihoon

MANTRA OF THE OPPRESSED

A Handbook of Creative Resistance

Mujeeb Jaihoon

Table of Contents

Freedom of Expression

Patriotism

Communal Harmony

Absolute Power

Coexistence

Communal Violenc

Selective Justice

Change

I Love India

Independence Day

Hypocritic Leaders

Power Politics

Hate Politics

Khatre mein hai

Jamia Attack

Godse Reborn

Judgment Day

True Spirituality

Dissent and Democracy

Holocaust

Religiosity

Mantra of Extremists

Introduction

In Mantra of the Oppressed, I have attempted to critically analyze the contemporary social and political conditions of the world and India in particular. Through poems, essays, and quotes, I discuss and evaluate India's arrest into autocracy. As an equally creative and intellectual enquiry, this collection brings empathetic examination to the extremist majoritarian influence. The book discusses the extent to which a fascist regime drastically impacts the ideas and livelihood of the present-day oppressed and marginalized minority communities in India.

The power of thought that's informed by personal reason can never be diminished by an intolerant governing force. Throughout each poem, essay, or spurred-on thought, readers will find that creativity is a catalyst for resistance.

Mantra of the Oppressed offers novel perspectives and artistic debates which decorate discussions of India's need for emancipation. While activists are jailed and homes of the oppressed are bulldozed, words and their ability to inform and inspire can never be controlled by another. I've come to understand this power, and my hope is for readers to find it for themselves too.

This handbook of creative resistance beckons its readers to open both their hearts and minds to an empathetic examination of India's current state of political affairs. The book deals with problematic and complex themes spanning a wide range of oppressive topics. From contemporary challenges and human rights violations, to the sad state of

Indian Muslims in particular, these pages command attention and encourage discussion.

From cover to cover, the fascist influence is colorfully criticized for killing the spirit of India's diversity as opposed to the freedom found in traditional Indian culture. What was once a powerful pluralist nation is now taking its descent into a land without dissent. These realities and reasons for resistance are presented through stories and anecdotes by blending poetry and prose with in-depth and intellectual essays and quotes.

Before present-day political issues become a history lesson on war and unrest, Mantra of the Oppressed strives to inspire immediate action through empathy and dialogue based on mutual respect and tolerance.

Mujeeb Jaihoon

January 01 2023

POEMS

Who will tame the Rogue Ztate?

Frustrated by global inaction to the daylight genocide in Palestine, the question arises: Who will contain the Zionist thug?

'We stand by the dead
    We support the displaced
    We succor the disabled
    We serve the deprived'

But who will tame the Rogue Ztate?
    Who will knock with the Mosaic Punch?
    Who will arrest the savage Thug?
    Who will pull their below rug?

While the civilized world
    Boils in this soup
    Who will stir the pot
    To injustice stop

Mujeeb Jaihoon

The Demons of Divisive Algorithms

*The hollow and shallow modern times have turned the storm
and calm equally deceptive.*

Neither left
    Nor right
    Neither liberal
    Nor fundamental
    Neither orthodox

Nor out of the box
    Hey, the demons
    Of divisive Algorithms
    Dream not to integrate
    Nor desire to segregate
    Within your greedy cobweb
    The hubb-harb of my sighing qalb.

Deceptive Storm and Calm

*The hollow and shallow modern times have turned the storm
and calm equally deceptive.*

Null thoughts
Numb touch
Blind vision
Void breath
Treacherous Time
Ruthless routine
Dispassionate dreams
Disloyal folks
Bombarding beeps
Audacious alerts
Deceptive the storm
Deceptive the calm
My empty mind-vessel:
Not even a slight sound
My Honey
And Moon
I reached to Get
But flew Away

Mujeeb Jaihoon

To the Disruptors without Alternatives

Disruptors who violently upset the status quo must come with better alternatives for their talks and actions to make any sense.

To those who destruct and demolish
　　The beautiful bridge
　　Hey, have you built
　　An alternative?

To those Who dismantle and disrupt
　　Successful institutions
　　Hey, have you established
　　An alternative?

To those who depose and dethrone
　　Visionary leaders and scholars
　　Hey, have you moulded
　　An alternative ?

Hey disruptors!

Alternatives are
　　The real game-changer
　　Else, Destruction is
　　Mere child's play.

The Commodified Existence

From distorted values to commodified minds, this poetic critique explores the modern societal decay.

Critics turned to cheerleaders
    Orators to actors
    Scholars to dollars
    And lions to lapdogs

Invaders illustrated as innocents
    And defenders defiled as devils
    Scams bundled as gifts
    Lust lauded as love

Paradise painted in properties
    Promises penned on melting papers
    Respect and reverence ridiculed
    Dignity deemed dysfunctional

Every art and thought
    Is sold and bought
    Every mind today a marketplace
    Human existence: mere merchandise.

Mujeeb Jaihoon

To the Popcorn-eating Enablers

*On the inaction of the silent bystanders as the poor continue
to be deprived of their right to life and liberty.*

As the weak are lynched
    And the homes are bulldozed
    As the Pens are penalized
    And the Nature is devastated

As the State sponsors the terror
    And the Fakir eclipses the Führer[1]
    As pogroms appear in daylight plunder
    And the Race-parasite leech-render

Woe to the popcorn-eating enablers
    Boo to the conformist collaborators

Shame on the complicit conspirators
    Damn on the silent bystanders

One day these goons will seek you out
    Your silence today will drive you then out
    The price of your indifference
    Will cost your peaceful lives

Embrace your conscience

---

[1] Führer is a German word meaning 'leader' or 'guide'. As a political title, it is
strongly associated with the Nazi dictator Adolf Hitler.

Mantra of the Oppressed

Chant for them a prayer
Invoke your courage
Inspire the Change

Mujeeb Jaihoon

Modern Men and Ancient Beasts: Kindred in Sounds and Actions

On the men and women who imitate the sounds of animals with their hostile and hateful actions towards fellow humanity.

Barking anchors
    Hissing preachers
    Roaring politicians
    Squeaking heroes

Howling colleagues
    Buzzing traders
    Meowing models
    Mooing lovers

Never in the world
    Were Men and Beasts
    In sound and actions
    So kindred together

Great Bigots Think Alike: Indian Muslima[2] to the Establishment

On Indian Muslim woman's response to her self-proclaimed patrons who exploit her pain and pride for their selfish motives.

For the Turban-headed Orthodox
    I am their headline of meets and seminars
    Yet, they keep me out of every stage
    And gloat about Islam's equality age

For the self-serving Extremists
    I am the trump card of revolution
    They appropriate my name and form
    To escalate their identity game

For the liberal Agnostic
    I am the eternal victim
    Of God and the Creed
    They see me with pain bleed

For the malefic Islamophobes
    I am the dreaded Mother Wolf
    Who reproduces day and night

---

[2] Feminine word for Muslim

To wipe out their endangered sheep

For the Corporate Brands
    I am yet another segment
    To sell the Hijab and Halal-brand
    I am their favorite guinea 'bitch'

For the con-Artist tribe
    I am their incredible imagination
    They sell my dreams and hopes
    But give no damn to my soul's essence

For the Sangh[3]-Wing bigots
    I am the oppressed slave
    Shedding crocodile tears

Only to realize their[4] Rashtra wet dreams

Hey you,
    The Establishment.
    You curb my rights
    Grab my choices
    Nab my books
    And then blab for my rights?

You know not a grain
    About my dreams or hopes
    And yet claim to be my patrons
    Exploiting my pain and pride

---

[3] Extreme Right Wingers in India

[4] Nation

You great bigots
    Think and brag alike
    But words without action:
    Everyone's piece of cake

Mujeeb Jaihoon

Quarantined Conscience

Regimes demand hearts to quarantine their conscience as throat-cutting trials continue for those who possess even a pinch of humanity.

Life has never been this 'light'
　　As not much is left of the 'Right'

The verdict of the Regime
　　Has eased further this game

'Keep only your IDs on hand;
　　Conscience
　　Justice
　　Dignity
　　Liberty
　　Leave them at home behind'

Celebrate this serfdom!
　　Flatter this fiefdom!

For,
　　Minimalistic:
　　The order of the day
　　Mechanistic:
　　The book of the play

Daylight Rape of Justice: Gandhari's Prayer for the Meerut Orphans

This is a poetic slam of State-sponsored brutalities. Gandhari,[5] the Vedic and virtuous queen of epic Mahabharata, decries the sufferings of the orphans in UP, India.

Gandhari once again
  Blindfolded[6] her glance
  Unable to bear the plight
  Of the Meerut Orphans

One hundred sons had she
  To bloody wars lost
  Since then had she became
  Every orphan's host

She shrieked for the orphans

---

[5] Gandhari plays a prominent role in the Hindu epic the Mahabharata. She was a princess of Gandhara and the wife of Dhritrashtra, the blind king of Hastinapura, and the mother of a hundred sons, the Kauravas, and a daughter. She is also considered as an archetype of virtue and moral strength.

[6] During her wedding, she had blindfolded herself in loyalty and solidarity with her blind husband.

Of Gulzar Road[7]
Their father, a laborer,
Was now dead

Thugs of the vengeful Tyrant
    Saw him a prey
    The boys still wait his return
    From work to play

She consoled the to-be-wed Saina
    Of the Shukkur Nagar
    Her father, dead now, unable to fulfill
    Her marital prayer

The 'Peacekeepers' had
    Unleashed their carnage

Showing no mercy nor justice
    To the young nor aged

She recalled her own agony
    When Imrana wept

'My orphaned babies have none
    To call their dad',
    Said the pregnant mother in tears–
    As she awaits the next orphan to be born

With Dhritarashtra[8] she shared
    The tale of Aleem

---

[7] This was the locality where the unfortunate incident occurred.

[8] Dhritarashtra was a Kuru king and the father of the Kauravas in the Hindu epic Mahabharata.

The baker who struggled
To see his kids smile

Bullets of hate
    Pierced his chest
    Batons of prejudice
    Struck his corpse

Peace: an unwanted corpse in Meerut
    Justice: molested at broad daylight

Gandhari, the queen
    Of virtue and the Pativratha[9]
    Cried foul at the guards
    Of the Fake-Devout:

"Justice is the slogan
    Of Bharat and Ram
    Compassion is the soul
    Of this kingdom

Saint-robed tyrants
    Will burn in hell
    Forever shall they
    In my curse dwell

---

[9] Fidelity

My soul is with those killed
    In haste, unjust
    My prayer is with those
    Who the victims assist

In Kanpur and Rampur,
    Let there be no fear
    In Lucknow and Sambhal
    Let peace prevail"

We are here to Forever Stay

The Indian Muslim will not faint and falter at the numeric altar of the regime – On the discriminatory Citizenship Amendment Bill 2019

You flatter the visiting guests
    At the Mahal[10]
    And feast on the Biryani,
    Kababs and jamuns

You flex your patriotic muscles
    At the Fort[11]
    And reign in the city
    Who the Sultans built

You gloat in Sherwani
    Hailing the Ghazal
    And flirt with your beloved
    In the Urdu vowel

You claim to be one nation-
    United by the folk of Babar
    India: whose very name
    Was donated by the 'Other'

---

[10] Taj Mahal built by the Mughal emperor, Shahjahan

[11] Red Fort, another Mughal-built monument.

Now, at last, when you have
    Had all the nectar
    You ask the Flower to prove
    Its love for the Garden!

We fought the Colonial Satan
    Tooth and nail
    We sacrificed our children
    For this dignified soil

Don't be fooled that your threat
    Will have us falter
    We shall remain firm:
    Not faint at your numeric altar

We are here to forever stay
    So, try not to keep us at bay
    Amend your thought and say
    And join us in peace and love play

To the Godless Goons of 'Mob India'

The bigots, who lynch and leech the weak, have total contempt for Rama Rajya, Mahatma Gandhi's non-violent utopia of mutual tolerance.

Lynch my body
    Pinch my soul
    Punch my pride
    Drench my blood

Staunch be your henchmen
    Bunch of bigoted hooligans
    Flinch us they from progress
    Wrench us they from justice

Exhaust every trick in your bag
    Pull every arrow off your quiver
    Bribe your cheerleaders forever
    Swing your dagger far and deeper

Destiny's Wheel will one day turn
    In your own inferno shall you burn
    Hate will then find no buyers
    Fade shall every Fake Soothsayers

Rama's Rajya will then re-assign
    Love and equality will re-reign
    Unity and Diversity will re-align
    Tolerance will again do India define

Mujeeb Jaihoon

23 Light Years: The Maryada of The Nation of Ram

Tribute to Abdul Gani Goni, a Kashmiri teacher, acquitted after illegally imprisoned for 23 years

Justice embarrassed
In the mirror of humanity
Patience wept
In the lap of forgiveness

A mother's heart
Scorched in the furnace of pain
For a glance of her son
Stolen by the Blind State

For 23 Light Years
A shallow story the State framed
Only to admit in the end
They had shamelessly erred

With neither personal vengeance
Nor legal recourse
That Son of India gifted
His foes with forgiveness

The Maryada[12] of the Nation of Ram,
    The Purushothaman[13]
    Is in forgiving the foe:
    So taught Kashmir's slandered teacher

---

[12] Etiquette

[13] Honored One

Mujeeb Jaihoon

Aporetic. Accursed: The Abyss of the Indian Muslim

On the political otherization of Muslims from mainstream Indian politics.

Buffooned as votebank
　　Blasphemed as venom

Lampooned on the big screen
　　Lambasted on the social timeline

Shattered in Corruption
　　Shredded by Communalization

Tested by the Dynastic Dukes
　　Tortured by Doctrinal Dictators

The choice for the Indian Muslim —
　　Aporetic at best, accursed at worst.

Roses are red: Violets are blood

Tribute to the 8-year-old girl, Asifa, who was 'kidnapped, starved, drugged, and raped repeatedly inside a Hindu temple' in Kathua, Jammu- India (January 2018).

As heroic as a holy martyr,
  She kindled pain and tear
  In the hearts of men and angels;
  Flying, then, like a fiery fairy-
  Ascended She into the skies …

Mujeeb Jaihoon

A Third of Triple

On the Triple-Talaq triumphant Indian Muslim women's appeal on the sad plight of her male relatives killed in mob lynching.

'They celebrate my win
    With joyful wine
    And wipe my tears
    As their pain

Such love showered
    On me as rain
    My own kin before them
    Like Cain

I have to my Triple-friends
    But one appeal
    True if your love is
    For my awful ordeal

If not triple, nor
    Even double be your feel

At least a third
    Of sympathy
    I beg for my kin
    They mob-kill'

Ghouta: Cultured Vultures, Uncivilized Vampires

A tribute to the two-year-old boy, Emir al-Bash, martyred in Ghouta, the war-torn suburb of Syria.

Monstrous mortars,
    Cold-numbed corpses,
    Saharan-dry eyes, and-
    Unfashionable funerals

Barada[14] waters turned to blood
    Anti-Libanus[15] became dead-mount
    A furnace of hell-like pain
    Ghouta has no uncommitted sin

Men and women here
    Simply shield and target
    For, Rulers and Rebels
    See not their souls

A lot so besieged
    Their chastity betrayed
    By the entire world-
    Ignobly Ignored

---

[14] A major river in Damascus

[15] Mountain range between Syria and Lebanon

Saw I there
    A woman in black
    Carrying a wrapped bag
    In blue bold case
    A slaughtered hunt
    Maybe it, I thought
    Little relief had she made
    In this drought

Asked I,

'What do you carry in that bag-
A lamb maybe or a deer of hunt?'

Replied She,
    Not lamb nor deer is this
    My son's remains but this is

He lived to see just years two
    Martyred by then sans a clue

Left home we
    In search of food
    Lest we find in market
    A good bite

Wells here have gone dry
    Olives here ooze more blood

He cried and cried to feed
    A mortar but struck him bleed

His soul to the Heaven flew unfed
    To be a Mother called I am ashamed

For the Lord I have no plea else
    But to feed my child in Heavens
    Angels be his playmates
    Rivers be his in his parks

In this land of curse and chaos
    Where insanity dances in streets

Vultures maybe of some culture
    Not so its vampire-vying tyrants

Hitler and Genghis be shocked
    At our onlookers' inanimate gaze

This beleaguered league
    Of bystanders
    United, but, with
    The beads of discord

Angel of Death may not have had
    A welcoming crowd as ours:
    Who tirelessly host
    His Death feast'

Mujeeb Jaihoon

Al Quds to Rest of the Muslim World: May Lord have Mercy on your Cowardice

Despite the atrocities of the Israeli forces on Palestinians, the world maintains a deafening silence vindicated only by cowardice

My bricks are battered
    My pillars are shattered
    My men are dying
    My children are crying

Yet I pray
    For your sake
    Your failure
    To humanely act

May Lord have mercy
    On your fear
    Exempt you from
    His justice-fire

Let Him not take
    You to task, for-
    To your Regimes
    You never ask

Your mouth and hands
    Are silently bound

With tags and likes
You are cozily abound

To suffer and suffocate
Has been my eternal fate

But did you
Ever contemplate:
What excuse
Shall you narrate?

Mujeeb Jaihoon

That Friday In Bangla[16] sang the Paradise-Bird

Tribute to Hosna Ara Parvin, the brave Bangladeshi lady martyr of the Christ Church terrorist attack, New Zealand, on Mar 15 2019.

The Daring Daughter
    Of the Lion of God[17]
    And Umm Ammara,[18]
    The heroine of Uhud[19]

Assembled near the gate
    Of 'the Abode'
    To welcome
    The 'Beautiful many-Starred'[20]

A fairy was she

---

[16] The language of Bangladesh.

[17] Zaynab, the grand-daughter of the Prophet Muhammad and daughter of Lady Fāṭima and Alī, known as the lion of Allah.

[18] A lady companion of the Prophet, is celebrated for her remarkable role in the Battle of Uhud, in which she sustained several wounds while protecting the Messenger of God.

[19] The site of the second battle between Muslim and unbelievers.

[20] Hosna, or the beautiful, and Parvin, referring to cluster of stars. One of the several martyrs who died in the white-supremacist terrorist attack in Christchurch shooting

In the tigress form
Leaped had she
To save her man, wheel-borne[21]

Embracing the dark venom
    Of the white-zealous
    Eclipsed she the courage
    Of thousand warriors

River Turag[22] began
    To dance in ways wild
    Baitul Makarrum[23] yearned
    For her selfless Sujud
    Boasted Hazrat Jalal[24]
    About this Pori[25]child
    That Friday, in Bangla sang
    The paradise bird

---

[21] Hosna's physically challenged husband, Faird, whom she had brought to the masjid on a wheelchair.

[22] The river in the outskirts of Dhaka, capital of Bangladesh.

[23] The 10th largest mosque in the world, capable of accommodating more than thirty thousand people, located in Bangladesh.

[24] Prominent Sufi mystic, Hazrat Shah Jalal, widely known for the propagation of Islam in Hindustan and Bengal.

[25] The Bangla equivalent for Pari, or fairy.

Mujeeb Jaihoon

Un-Evolved

*Despite transformation in all creatures including the virus,
men & women adamantly continue their old habits.*

The queen and her bees
  Rivers of honey hived

Winds and skies too
  Into new worlds revolved

The whales and sharks
  Into deeper oceans dived

Nay, the vigilante virus
  Into vile variants evolved

Men and women
  In habits remain same

In greed are they proud
  In hate are they loud
  Enslaved to the 'Cloud'
  Severed from their Lord

It's OK to be a Human

In this glossy era deluded with superhuman success stories, sometimes it is worthwhile to remain just an innocent human.

You don't have to win
    All the time
    It ok to lose sometimes
    It's OK

You don't have to find the way
    In every journey
    It's OK to get lost sometimes
    It's OK

You don't need to be loved
    And liked forever
    It's ok to be ignored at times
    It's OK

You don't need to be among friends
    And folks always
    It's ok to be alone
    It's OK

You don't need to be strong
    And cunning always
    It's ok to be fooled, sometimes
    It's OK

You don't need to laugh
   And smile always
   It's ok to cry and weep some times
   It's OK

It's ok to be human
   And stay human,
   Always.

The New Year Prayer

Lofty hopes keep the humanity in prayers as the past year elopes paving the way for another new year

As the past year subtly elopes
    Dawns the New with lofty hopes
    With prayers for ease of pains
    And joy upon the human face
    Count over count our Age seeps
    And towards the End, life leaps
    We yearn for a Messiah of Peace
    Our tears who with love wipes

ESSAYS

Hijab Ban: The Surgical Strike on Tolerance and Individual Freedom

Hijab, long criticized as an instrument of patriarchal oppression, has inadvertently won the hearts of many critics

The recent Hijab row in Karnataka points to larger social malaise getting wider traction across India and that inadvertently might pose irreparable damage to the idea of nation guaranteed by the Indian Constitution. This unconstitutional encroachment is a brazen continuation of the alarming trend of hate attacks against minorities and Dalit communities with total impunity. The changing politics in the country after 2014 has ushered in assertive militant and masculine majoritarianism. Revenge politics espoused by Hindutva right wing political parties and cultural organizations are on a spiral path with stoic silence of State apparatus pandering to the cause of growth of contempt.

Intolerance Reloaded

The Hijab Ban is latest in strings of anti-Muslim campaigns. CAA protests precipitated an identity crisis among the beleaguered Muslims. It follows after the misogynistic episodes of 'Sulli Deals' and 'Bulli Bai' and the hate mongering Haridwar Dharma Sansad. Even the Triple Talaq Bill has produced a counter result as Muslims are opposing reforms due to fear of abrogation of personal law to bring uniformity at the cost of famed Indian diversity.

Karnataka has long become a laboratory for BJP to test waters to make a frontal gush to other south Indian states. Besides Goa, nowhere else in South India has BJP grown into credible electoral power and hence every development in Karnataka would have wider ripple effects across the region. The domino effects are already palpable with various BJP-ruled states contemplating similar curbs on Hijab in educational institutions.

'Indianness' at Stake

Dietary preferences were attacked earlier as violent mob lynching claimed several lives. The freedom to hold Friday congregation prayers was also infringed. The compromise deal in the Babri Masjid verdict rendered the existence of Muslims more tenuous. These attacks should not be misjudged squarely as attacks on one community long accused of being a generous recipient of appeasement politics. When the rights to honorable existence and religious freedom are trampled upon, the first casualties are the idea of 'Indianness' espoused by the framers of the Constitution and the exquisiteness of religious pluralism.

Hijab Ban: Bane on Women Education

In Karnataka, when Muslim women are heckled and restricted from entry to educational institutions, it is a gross violation of Article 21 (A) which promises Right to Education. Because Muslim women are the late entrants to higher education, the denial of education to them will aggravate backwardness among the community. BJP, which often projects itself as the liberator of Muslim women, should ensure the seamless education of Muslim women adhering to their religious choices.

Hijab: Not Overnight Fad

Hijab has been a central part of the Muslim female identity for centuries. Both the traditional Muslim women and her modern counterparts consider this apparel more than a mere identity apparel. Unlike the Saffron Shawl, unheard of in traditional Hindu commoner's spirituality, Hijab is not an overnight political fad invented for communal indulgence.

Hijab Ban: Blessing in Disguise

Incidentally, the Hijab Row has also proved to be a blessing in disguise for the battered Faith. The Community has been receiving praise and prayers from across the political and intellectual spectrum. Hijab, which used to be criticized as a patriarchal instrument of oppression, has inadvertently won the hearts of some the most fervent critics. Many have also hailed the brave heart Muslim women who fought the 'Saffron thugs' as role models of courage and resistance.

Hijab: The Unapologetic Expression and Assertion

Donning Hijab isn't identity politics or jingoism. It is rather an unapologetic expression and assertion of the new Indian Muslim female, ready to take on the majoritarian regime that fear the rise of the educated and empowered Muslim woman.

Soul Searching is wanted

Notwithstanding the legal and political support for the Hijab, the Faithful also need to undergo soul searching to explore the spiritual and moral context behind this predicament. Community needs to ponder on the poverty of political and social leadership which encourage the miscreants to violate the right and freedom of the Faithful, which are enshrined in the Constitution. The call for community representation in law, legal and legislation has not received adequate response so far.

Political Marginalization Drives Legal Conservatism among Indian Muslims

Muslim community should be encouraged to take internal reforms without State compulsion

Amid the existential crises of Indian Muslims after Partition, the constitutional assurances given to the collective identity was vital in ameliorating the fears of the Muslim community. While individual freedoms are tenable while interpreting the constitution, recognition of the collective identity of the Muslim community by the way of State protection for colonial era Muslim Personal Law and special powers for minority institutions helped integrate Muslims in the fledgling Nation.

When the Nehru government feverously pushed the agenda of codification Hindu Code, Muslims were spared. Nehru was of the opinion that Muslims being an embittered minority, the State shall not force changes in Personal Law and; instead support all community-led reform movements. His was a prudent political act to forestall militant community mobilization.

As pointed out by Muhamed Qasim Zaman, Muslims in Indian subcontinent were aware of the colonial nature of the Muslim Personal Law and an undercurrent of reform was prevalent among the Faithful. It was Ashraf Ali Thanawi who fiercely endorsed flexibility and contemporary changes in Muslim Personal Law to shake off imperialist connotation of Muslim Laws. Scholars like Justice Ameer Ali, Asaf A. Fayzee, and Muhammed Ismail Sahib were aware of the legal changes in contemporary Muslim communities and the vested interests of Colonial powers in feudalizing legal cannon of Islam. The Muslim Shariat Act of 1937 and Marriage Dissolution Act of 1939 were in fact nascent steps towards gradual progression towards modernization and codification of Muslim law in the Subcontinent.

According to Zoya Hassan, the political insecurity after Partition led to an abrupt halt to the codification of Muslim Law and, instead, the identity fears of the Community manifested in their staunch support to Colonial era Personal Laws. It was viewed as a final concession to Indian Muslims and hence to be safeguarded at any cost. Modernization and codification were relegated to the backburner for the protection of limited constitutional rights. Narendra Subramanian has documented the role of Personal Laws in the formation of Muslim identity in India.

Era of Community-Led Internal Reforms

The relative immunity from State intervention expedited internal reform in the community. The jolt of reality in independent India accentuated the pace of internal reforms. Staring at the bleak reality of Indian Muslims, community leaders, cutting across various factions, supported internal reforms in varying degrees. Women education was promoted. Women visibility in formal and informal sectors was motivated. Hadeeth literature was studied to reform existing Muslim canonical laws.

The general reading of Indian Muslims as a monolithic community often glosses over the vibrant diversity underlying the regional differences in Indian Islam. Among South Indian Muslims, due to historical reasons, internal reforms were at meteoric rise whereas the North Indian counterpart took a lackadaisical approach. While elite upper caste Muslims sensed opportunity in the scarce crumbs the new republic threw to them, other marginalized sections of the society soon appropriated internal reform thanks to evolving situations.

Secular education got wider acceptance among the community. Madrassas and Maktabs, established exclusively for religious education, showed promising interest in integrating school education. Many states enacted laws with the consensus of the Community. The induced reforms with the blessings of the community were making substantial strides in reforming the community. And with the Shah Bano case all hell broke loose.

The Shah Bano issue of 1980s changed the course of Muslim reform movements. The conservative and reactionary clergy tightened their grip on the Community. Progressive sections were relegated into irrelevance. Major concessions by the Rajiv Gandhi government to the conservative section by overruling the Supreme Court verdict proved fatal for the progress of the Community.

Rise of Hindutva Politics and Increasing Legal Conservatism among Muslims

The failure of the Janata Government initially laid the foundation for Hindutva politics. Later, Mandal politics inflamed religious passion and Kamandal politics surrounding Babari Masjid only hastened the growth of right wing Hindutva politics. They questioned the alleged minority appeasement politics. Major war cry of BJP was to end state protection to Muslim Personal Law. According to BJP, the existence of separate civil laws for Muslims is against the unity of nation and demanded the implementation of Uniform Civil Code.

Along with recurring communal tensions, the waning political importance as a key vote bank pushed the community into defense. This had a debilitating impact on the orientation of the community. While political changes of Muslim community are well-documented, the question of how it perpetuates legal conservatism needs keen attention. Afraid of Hindutva attacks on 'Muslimness', a general trend of dogmatic loyalty towards Muslim Personal Law could be seen.

After 2014, when Modi captured Delhi for the first time in Indian electoral politics without Muslim support, a sense of obscurantism has overwhelmed the community. The Hindutva rhetoric denigrating the honorable partnership of Muslims with the Republic has raised existential threats among the faithful. Citizenship controversies further alienated the Muslims. Muslims generally are suspicious of

Hindutva hidden agendas of undermining constitutional support in their future nation with majoritarian zeal.

Even Muslims are not averse to the idea of reforming the religious laws as happened in many other Islamic countries. But the fear of Hindutva has practically stalled community-led internal reforms. While BJP heralds Triple Talaq Bill as a milestone in ensuring justice for Muslim women, the community was scornful of the act while the practice is increasingly condemned by the faithful. Making a civil act a criminal offense which invokes imprisonment, the community has serious reservation about the ulterior motives of the BJP in forcing changes in Muslim laws. Gazala Wahab has discussed the dilemma among Muslims in supporting reforms pushed by BJP.

Religious identities are calling shots these days instead of caste loyalties. Muslim community should be encouraged to take internal reforms without State compulsion. Civil society, religious leadership and educated sections have to play bigger roles in reforming the Colonial era Muslim Personal Laws. But, imposition of State-led top-down approach will hurt the pace of internal reforms of Muslim community. Reforms should be the outcome of community-led process. The State shall merely aid the reform and every effort to shove down changes ought to have adverse results.

God is with the Oppressed

True Ramarajya[26] will only entitle Muslims to greater peace, equality and freedom. Nevertheless, patience is indispensable.

Darker Black Days

Yet another Black day for the Indian Muslims in their identity struggle. Aug. 05. of 2019 and 2020 will go down in history, like Dec. 06. 1992, as unfortunate days when the founding fathers of this nation will be turning in their graves. Indian Muslims are an unfortunate lot who voluntarily chose to stay back in this country, even as a large portion of their faith fraternity migrated to the newly founded 'Holy State'. They took this stand with calculated risks, knowing well they would forever remain an endangered minority in every sense of the word- political, religious and cultural.

As law-abiding citizens of the much-celebrated largest democracy in the world, Indian Muslims have time and again bore the brunt of majoritarian politics. The secular and Left wing spectrum have repeatedly taken them for rides, well aware of the community's fear of the Right wing. Loyalty of

---

[26] The country as perceived by Lord Ram. Mahatma Gandhi's non-violent utopia of mutual tolerance.

Muslims has been rewarded with institutional insult and indifference at best, and betrayal at worst.

Despite upon Despite Verdict

The Nov, 09, 2019 verdict of the honorable Supreme Court regarding the disputed land – claimed by Hindus as the birthplace of Lord Ram and by Muslims as site of Babri Masjid built during Mughal times – was a complete shock to many sane minds. Despite acknowledging that there is no evidence of a temple pre-existed the mosque and therefore no temple was destroyed for the mosque construction, despite admitting that demolition of the Babri Masjid was a criminal act, despite accepting that act of placing an idol in the Babri Masjid in 1949 as an 'act of desecration' – the verdict was pronounced in favor of the 'Other' to pacify majoritarian aspirations. That's like declaring the runner-up as the champion, not the actual winner, to respect the sentiment of the spectators.

There is little historical or legal proof that any temple was actually demolished to construct a mosque. That remains a controversy. But it is modern history that the mosque was razed in broad daylight- under the nose of the police and army, in the watchful eyes of the media and under the inaction of the administration.

Evict us, Insult us, But Can't Erase us

True, every Indian Muslim is hurt and wounded by the chest-thumbing rumble of the supremacist Sangh brigade. Their patriotism has received yet another blow from this hitherto tolerant and inclusive nation. But this is not the end of the Indian Muslim project.

Every Muslim problem is ultimately their spiritual problem. A Muslim can be a Muslim, only if he or she firmly believes that the God they worship aligns with the weak and oppressed, not the egoistic elite nor the repressive regime. No doubt, Muslims have been unjustly wronged, like in the past, on this black day as the leader of the country inaugurated this 'funeral' of Indian secularism. The patience and restraint of Indian Muslims are well documented. Muslims have lived and prospered in India long before 1528, when the Babri Masjid was built. Their timeline continued unaffected even after Dec. 06. 1992 when the structure was demolished by the Karsevak[27] mob with the blessing of the Establishment. And now with the Bhumipujan ceremony (Aug. 05. 2020), they may be hurt, insulted and wounded, but not non-existent. Day in and day out, many have been killed in mob lynching and communal riots. The majoritarian regime may be racing to evict and erase the Muslim identity from history and national identity. But the Muslim will remain an integral part of India's legacy; past, present and future.

The modernist Ataturk Inc. converted many mosques to bars and museums, banned beards, caps and Hijabs; jailed the Ulama and shut down Madrassas. But tables turned within a few decades. Modern Turkey is the perfect example of the anti-climax for Islamophobic ambitions. The Hindutva-

---

[27] RSS activists

dominated Indian regime hasn't even come close as Ataturk did.

Muslim Maryada in Gandhi's Ramarajya

There is no nothing shameful or embarrassing to Muslims for the construction of a temple in honor of Ram, an important legend in the Indian traditions, symbolic of justice, forgiveness and dignity- values which are central to a Muslim's spiritual salvation.

In the words of Gandhi, the father of Nation murdered by a Hindu fanatic: "By Ramarajya I do not mean Hindu Raj. I mean by Ramarajya, Divine Raj, the Kingdom of God... I acknowledge no other God but the one God of truth and righteousness. Whether Rama of my imagination ever lived or not on this earth, the ancient ideal of Ramarajya is undoubtedly one of true democracy in which the meanest citizen could be sure of swift justice without an elaborate and costly procedure".

As a practicing Muslim, I unapologetically believe that Ramarajya, as envisioned by Gandhiji, will only entitle my Muslim countrymen to greater peace, equality and freedom. Nevertheless, Patience will be indispensable, like those of Turkish men and women during Ataturk times, in this mission to overcome the momentary existentialist challenges.

Empathy is at the heart of Multi-Faith Camaraderie of Anti-CAA Protests

Had the Indian Muslims reciprocated the same solidarity for the oppressed Dalits as others who are aggressively standing for Muslims now?

Faith and Trials are Complementary

Muslims are a time-tested lot: they have historically faced several existentialist tests in their march across the annals of history. Threats and tortures, hardships and harassments are not strangers to this Faithful lot. Since its inception, trials have been chasing this fiercely Monotheistic Faith like a shadow. In fact, the Holy Quran almost construes Faith and Trails as complementary. Sufism, or higher spiritual Islam, attributes deeper faith with greater trials to test the perseverance.

The Fight for Hate-free India

Nevertheless, Indian Muslims are petrified with the biased NRC and CAA laws enacted by the majoritarian regime skewed by the Hindutva ideology. Small children are suffering from poor mental health conditions due to this discriminatory citizenship-related legislation. With past already tarnished in popular culture, uncertainty now hangs over their present and future as well.

The Indian Muslims have a greater responsibility to reclaim the spirit of secular India, for, it is their very presence which helps to sustain the much celebrated definition of the country's secular ethos. Yes, it means making sacrifices in their struggle against the Majoritarian Regime. Yes, it means staging indefinite protests on streets and institutions. Yes, it means mobilizing their creative genius in every way possible. However, it does not mean giving up, for, the future hate-free India will kiss the feet of these men and women who fought bigotry tooth and nail, despite seeing no light at the end of tunnel rife with turmoil.

Saluting Non-Muslim Camaraderie

The Indian Muslims may not hesitate in joining hands with fellow faith communities who have shown unparalleled solidarity with their Muslim brethren. Admittedly, it is not easy for the members of the non-Muslim community, especially the Hindu brothers and sisters, whose gadget screens are persistently bombarded with Muslim-hating audio-visual memes. Moreover, the intimidating pressure from their family and friends' circles isn't mellow either.

Therefore, Muslims have to respect and salute the camaraderie of fellow faith communities, who risk their mental peace and social ties for the sake of saving the secular spirit of the Nation. The lower caste segments have been suffering from social injustice, molestation and lack of opportunities for ages. Have the Indian Muslims shown the same solidarity with them as other communities are showing towards Muslims now? This question begs for reflection and perhaps correction from the part of many who are wailing about injustice and indifference. For, God has set Justice free from the shackles of communal and racial tags.

Mujeeb Jaihoon

Shaheen Bagh:
The Magnificent Spirit of India

Shaheen, meaning falcon, and Bagh, the garden of diversity, represents the true spirit of Indian heritage of secularism and pluralism.

We need to ponder about this beautiful phrase called Shaheen Bagh. Shaheen stands for falcon, a huge magnificent bird which soars in the skies. As our beloved poet Allama Iqbal wrote,

Tu Shaheen hai,
Parwaaz hai kaam Tera

You are a falcon and your task is to fly higher.

India is a magnificent and powerful country which has a heritage and civilizations dating back to thousands of years.

Bagh means garden where different flowers bloom; not just one. It stands for different faiths, different belief systems and political opinions. We have historically addressed India as Gulistan, which is the same as Bagh.

Shaheen Bagh is the very spirit of Indian citizenship. Surely, we are becoming part of history as we join the Shaheen Bagh Square (Protest) at Calicut in solidarity with our Northern brothers and sisters. Shaheen Bagh is all that India stands for.

The Coronavirus, which presumably originated from the powerful China, is eating up the entire world. Until recently, everybody wanted to do business with the most competitive economy in the world. But this tiny virus has created havoc in China and its economy is shivering. So never judge anything by its size. 'Shaheen Bagh', which may seem to be a harmless minority protest, is the Corona virus that may eat up the Sangh Parivar brigade and their goons who are killing the very spirit of India.

We, as the Indian Muslims, perhaps have a bigger claim on our heritage than others. The very name India is the contribution of the Arab world, from the word 'al Hind'. A few days back, the most powerful man in the world, the president of the United States, had visited our great country. He chose the Taj Mahal to take selfie with his wife. Likewise, the Israeli PM chose the same Mughal-built monument to take a selfie.

The Taj and many other monuments such as the Red Fort, where India celebrates the Republic Day, prove that we are the locals of this country and those who accuse us as foreigners are the ones who have to prove their belonging to this land. These are contributions of the Muslim civilization which make us Indians first and we shall always remain Indians.

(Talk at the Shaheen Bagh Square (Indefinite Protest – Feb 01 2020 onwards)

Mujeeb Jaihoon

Anti-CAA University Protests: Writing on the Wall for Vegetable Politicians, Lapdog Media & Selfie Celebrities

Historically, the fate of divisive rulers and their doormats have been suicidal at best.

Popcorn Time for India's Adversaries

India's enemies are having the time of their lives now: eating popcorn while watching the theatrics of political unrest sweeping across the largest democracy in the world. Indians and her economy are burning at the hands of its fascist regime, leaving the 'infiltrating spy intelligence' of hostile neighbors literally jobless. India, envied till recently for its secular and tolerant heritage, is passing through one of its darkest nights while the sun of fascism is shining at its brightest.

Barbaric Trespass

The widespread protests against the Citizenship Amendment Act (CAA) across the country's university campuses have evoked nationwide response against the brute use of force on the student community. The security forces barbarically trespassed into classrooms, wrecked libraries and damaged prayer rooms inside the campus. Visuals of students with smashed eyes and bleeding heads are forcing the public to question the very intent of those responsible for maintaining law and order. The student fraternity of Jawaharlal Nehru University, Indian Institute of Technology Mumbai, Banaras Hindu University came out on the streets in solidarity with those afflicted in Jamia Millia Islamia and Aligarh Muslim University.

National Solidarity

The most violent protests were witnessed in 'minority-branded' campuses, claim the cheerleaders of the ruling regime. However, that does not explain the logic behind the state-wide protests in Assam, the north-eastern region, where non-Muslim ethnic peoples are on the streets against the CAA. Nevertheless, the unprecedented protests by the apolitical citizens have a certain message for the influential elites of the country.

Vegetable Politicians

Firstly, for the Vegetable Politicians, who refused to participate in the popular uprisings have their days numbered. Leading politicians, from the Left and Right, reduced their response to tweets and posts on their egomaniac timelines. It was the students who unabatedly bled and defended their colleagues without any support from the prominent politicians. Despite being home to several national leaders, not a single Parliamentarian in Delhi rushed to rescue the students from State-sponsored atrocities. The public, hopefully, will not forget the inaction of these vegetable politicians and this fiasco may give rise to a new brand of brand-less student leaders in the future, thus reshaping the political landscape of the country.

Lapdog Media

Secondly, the Media who either ignore the countrywide protests or treacherously tweak the narrative according to their vested interests are going to pay a huge price for their lapdog loyalty to the regime. Their partisan portrayal makes them partners in crime against the popular resentment brewing against the Establishment. Citizen journalism will soon break the spine of biased mainstream reporting.

Selfie Celebrities

Thirdly, the celebrities— from film, music or sports— who built their stardom with the emotional bricks of fanatic admirers, have turned a deaf ear to the cry of the student community. Despite many stars being alma mater of leading campuses affected by the bloody protests, they chose to remain silent cheerleaders of the oppressive regime. There was a time when it was considered fashionable to be anti-government. However, these stars have lost their 'glitter' of conscience as they vie for the selfie with the 'Divisive Lord'.

Once, Twice, But Not Always

The strategy of the Fascists has always been to chop the leg if it doesn't fit the shoe. They may be successful once, twice but not always. History will not forgive those bigots who failed India and her secular ideals. The fate of those who divide the people on the basis of religion or race have been suicidal at best. The same has been true for those doormats who served them for vested interests.

To the Fascists:
Proudly Indian, Proudly Muslim

On Citizenship Amendment Bill 2019

Hey Fascists! Lord chose India to be my love at first sight as soon as I opened my eyes to this world. No law on earth can amend or blind that reality. No lawmakers can forsake my right with whatever bill they pass.

Hey Fascists! The choice of my homeland is by divine decree, not by anyone's favor. So look elsewhere for a better victim to pursue your nasty power play.

Love will triumph and partisan hate and bigotry will be defeated soon.

For, I am proudly Muslim, I am proudly Indian.

Purging India's Religious Beast for Greater Humanity: Challenges and Opportunities

The Nation is on the verge of a catastrophic implosion if the megawatts of Religiosity go unchecked, unbridled.

Sind. Hind. India

As we all know, India is named after the Sindhu river, after the Arabs changed the first syllable to 'H' which ultimately became Hind. Indians are, thus, incredibly indebted to the Arabs' and Persians' innocent misarticulation which is how we reached the Anglican form, India.

India: Sacred Games of Indigenous Identity

The biggest debate happening in the country today revolves around the true legacy of a real Indian. Every community, state or religious class has their own legitimization for this identity challenge. It is impossible to liberate the spirit of India from the body of religion, or vice versa.

India is essentially a religious beast. There is a nuclear reactor of religiosity or religious identity within the majority of Indians today. The Nation is on the verge of a catastrophic implosion if these megawatts of identity-energy go unchecked and untamed. An unbiased observer can easily notice religion in every aspect of Indian popular culture. Movies, music, books and politics celebrate (read manipulate) religion as an integral component. Every mess, literal or otherwise, we see today is done in the name of religion.

Religion inspires Civilization too

But it is equally true that religion has within it as much noble energy to inspire charity, build homes for the poor, run educational institutions and architecture besides others. Many temples, mosques and churches are landmark contributions to our civilization. The greatest awe-inspiring architectural monument which generates the highest tourism dollars for the Nation is neither a secular nor political building. Rather, one which is designed after an apparent religious symbol.

Secular by Constitution; Religious by Action

India is indeed a secular nation by constitutional definition. Nevertheless, at heart, its legacy is blatantly religious. Religion cannot be divorced from Indian public life. Else, movies did not have to start with messages and animations depicting gods or goddesses or even a 'Thank God.'

Agreeable Discourse between Disagreeable Humans

Religion is essentially meant to be a private discourse between humans and God. Let us, in these troubled times, also attempt to transform it into an agreeable discourse between disagreeable humans. This would only help to clear the fog of ignorance and misunderstanding. Let spiritualists of different faiths talk to one another. For, hate does not take courage. Love does. Amicable exchange of talks between interfaith believers will help to kill violence.

Extremism is the fruit of Ignorance

There are extremists in almost every organization. Let the extremists of one Faith show the guts to have an open discussion with the fanatics of another. If not in public, then at a confidential place, for candid exchange of ideas. In fact, ignorance is at the heart of one's allegiance to extremism.

Even if the discourse between the religious leadership — priests, Pundits and Ulama — fails, only a few hours of talk may be wasted. But if it wins, the Nation can be saved from hell on earth. That will be a victory for all faiths. For, religion strives to save humanity from hell — before and after death too.

(From a book talk at Jamia Millia Islamia, New Delhi, on Sep 29, 2018.)

Mujeeb Jaihoon

Hate for Humanity and Faith in God Cannot Co-exist

Whatever be the hateful and painful provocation, our Faith does not sanction us to respond with sweeping hate and bigotry.

Hunger remains the greatest motivator in the world. The feast of breaking fast brings unimaginable joy for the believers. Community Iftars are thus humanitarian milestones because it tackles the hunger of the common lot with a devotional spirit.

Hate and bigotry have become ubiquitous around us. On the streets and neighborhoods, hate has begun to reign unabated. Moreover, hate is also spreading through social media and personal messaging platforms.

Brothers in Faith...

Islam is built on the foundations of love and compassion. Whatever be the hateful and painful provocation, our Faith does not sanction us to respond with sweeping hate and bigotry. Indeed, hatred for humanity and Faith in God cannot co-exist.

We should take a pledge in this Holy Month to never ever share any hateful messages which violate our faith's teachings and hurt the dignity of fellow humanity.

(Talk at a Community Iftar held in Sharjah, Ramadan 2022)

Mujeeb Jaihoon

Nation-Building: Civility is the True Identity of a Muslim

Tipu Sultan, upon whose death the colonialists proclaimed – 'From today on, India is ours', has left behind a legacy for his community to uphold.

Dunya and Akhira

Islam is perhaps the only faith system in the world which honors the spiritual and bodily needs in beautiful proportions. The Quran has apportioned a great amount of verses regarding the observation and appreciation of Allah's signs from Nature. Dunya (temporal world) is as significant as Akhira (afterlife) in the discourse of religion of Allah. Ibada (devotion) encompasses the struggle of both worlds.

The Ummah Project

Muslims have always had to undergo existential struggles throughout history. They have never had couch potato moments in their journey. Indian Muslims are going through one of the toughest times in this country. It only shows that the Ummah Project is a continuous work in progress until the Last Day.

Nation Building: Reliving Tipu's Legacy

Muslim rulers and heroes who ruled India and fought the colonial nemeses may have faded from our sight. But that does not mean India stopped belonging to us. Tipu Sultan, upon whose death the Colonial Satan proclaimed – 'From today on, India is ours', has left behind a legacy of patriotism and loyalty for his community to uphold. India belongs to us, and we are obliged and responsible to build this country. Nation building does not mean building monuments nor boarding the bandwagon of power politics alone. Rather, it denotes becoming a good human being building peace between fellow countrymen.

Education and Discipline

Islam is not a private property of any tribe or race. It is the Almighty's gift for humanity at large. The best tools for nation building are education and discipline. Ibada, or devotional practices, includes our contribution to building the nation too.

For instance, one of you notices a stone or brick in the middle of the road as you were riding a cycle across the street. Islam expects its believers, even with an iota of faith, to remove such harmful obstacles so that no human being of any creed nor any beast get hurt. Islam is foremost a feast of reaching welfare, irrespective of their caste or creed.

Extending further this rationale, it would be ideal to say that safe driving is also part of a believer's worship. Bystanders should be able to identify a Muslim's vehicle from the style of his or her driving pattern. Abiding by public safety rules is part of a Muslim's attaining salvation. Violation of public safety rules is no less than Zulm, or transgression. Jumping a red signal is hence a spiritual sin as far as the ethical outlook of a Muslim is concerned.

Muslims are a breed of patience. While half of our belief is patience, we should exhibit Himalayan forbearance in face of the endless trials and injustice we may encounter in our daily life.

Nation building should be an act of love. Only if you love your creation will you exert sincerely for its well being. India or Hind is a land which comforted our Holy Prophet with a 'cool breeze'. Hence, we have every right and duty to make sure this nation enjoys progress and prosperity.

While patience is half of faith, we should correlate it with the Prophetic tradition, 'Love of one's nation is part of faith'. Our civility is our true identity, not merely our ethnic costumes.

(From a talk at Darul Huda Hangal Centre, Gejjihalli, Karnataka. Feb 20 2019.)

India is the Garden of Pluralism: Not a Graveyard of Monoculture

The demonic and despotic monoculture has to be uprooted from the Indian soil before it turns the nation to a monstrous zombie land.

Freedom struggle

The Indian nation did not win freedom by simply signing on some dotted lines, as in the case of a property transfer deal nor was it as cozy as a smartscreen swipe. Precious lives were lost, selfless sacrifices were made, life imprisonment were sentenced, houses and places of worship were razed down, wives became widows and children orphans. Indian independence will forever remain an unparalleled chapter in the book of human sufferings. Patience too.

Freedom in the cage of Post-Independent India

Yet, despite securing freedom from a foreign power, the battle for life and dignity continues for the common men and women. While European soccer teams are dominated and credited for their players from immigrant backgrounds, the Dalits of India– the children of God in the words of Gandhi – are yet to make their mark in the national cricket team.

Oppression in the name of caste and faith has taken a new turn in recent years. There is a deliberate attempt to blemish the secular soul of modern India, despite all its technological advancements and scientific progress which had more or less unified and inspired its diverse population. Some maniac minds and horrific hands are constantly conspiring to incite venom and hatred in the minds of citizens.

Pluralism and diversity are at the heart of 'Indianness'. Freedom of expression is the inevitable fuel that propels Indian democracy. Safety and security of women are hallmarks of any civilized society. Protection of the environment from the gluttonous corporate vultures is essential for the progressive and healthy future of the nation.

Midnight Street Dogs Safer than Daylight Indian Women

Unfortunately, the recent state of affairs is depicting almost completely a different picture. Non-sycophantic journalists are mercilessly murdered or intimidated. Whistle-blowers can no longer breathe fearlessly. Shockingly, street dogs roaming at midnight may be feeling safer than women and children in daylight.

One step for Kerala is a giant leap for India

The social and communal equation in Kerala is relatively different from other parts of India, especially the North. The secular fabric of Keralites is long established, despite some minor challenges in the recent past. Perhaps, that is the reason why a prominent Delhi-based journalist tweeted, 'what Kerala does today, India should do tomorrow'.

I would like to propose before this august audience the following initiatives for the consideration of Kerala government and its peoples:

1. Tourism

Kerala has numerous monuments of historical and spiritual significance of all denominations. The three major temples with magnificent architectural and devotional aura- Sabarimala Sastha Temple, Sivagiri Temple and Srikrishna Temple- are already tourist hotspots. However, authorities are yet to capitalize on other monuments, which will help bring both name and money to the Southern State. Even those oft-visited pilgrimage centers need to be promoted as the true HQ of Hindu spirituality in contrast to the extremist interpretation by the fanatics. This will promote Kerala as the true haven of religious tolerance and diversity.

2. Education

Kerala, with its cent percent literacy, boasts of several educational institutions with a powerful secular legacy. However, for reasons of poor infrastructure and mismanagement, they are yet to figure at the National level. The influx of Kerala students to other states is way more than inflow. This has to be reversed, urgently.

3. Media

Kerala Media scape, though include some of the brightest scribes and 'mouths' in the industry, suffer from the language barrier which overshadows their talent from those in the 'national' mainstream. The secular Malayali media houses, especially visual, have to adopt English programming to fight the communal narrative, which dominates many, if not all, the national channels.

Choosing between Gulistan vs. Qabristan

Monoculture is demonic and despotic. This venomous weed has to be uprooted from the Indian soil before it turns India to a monstrous zombie land. India is at its best as multicultural Gulistan (garden), not a fascist Qabristan (graveyard). We, the children of this nation, have a duty to ensure our country remains intact in its quintessential spirit.

QUOTES

Mob Lynching

"

Herbivore on the dining table. Carnivore on the streets. What name shall history call you?

83

Fascist Enablers

"

The brightest engineers and scientists in Germany were once Hitler's cheerleaders.

Hope

❝

*The hope of the believer
is stronger than the
reality of the weak.*

Freedom of Expression

"

*'Tragic' Comedy Shows
and 'Comic' Hate
Speeches. Missing
my irony-free India.*

Patriotism

"

*Despite all their
differences, the Mother
is dear to all her
children and vice versa.*

Communal Harmony

"

*Reinventing one's
spiritual traditions
is the only way to
safeguard communal
harmony.*

Absolute Power

"

*Constitutional
Amendments are the
illegitimate bedfellows
of Absolute
Power-Lovers.*

Coexistence

"

The birthplace of deities should not become graveyards of humans.

Communal Violenc

66

These vile vipers vying to vindicate their visceral venom for vicious vendetta. God save the Nation.

Selective Justice

66

*Indian Activists are
now indicted based
more on Nouns than
Verbs.*

Change

"

Yesterday's taboo is today's yahoo. Woe to the 'table-turns' in the feast of history.

I Love India

“

My nation. My passion. You will remain poets' elation despite the threats & tribulations.

Independence Day

"

*The Day when
India and Pakistan
can fearlessly wish
each other on their
Independence Days will
be the day when they
actually won freedom.*

Hypocritic Leaders

"

*Chameleon-In
Chief.*

Power Politics

"

Principles are no more than Tissue Paper in the Power-pocket of a Politician.

Hate Politics

"

*Woe to the Merchants
of Hate. Wow to the
Saints of Love.*

Khatre mein hai

"

Raja aur mantri aapke
Sipahi aur bandook bhi
Na jaane phir bhi kyon
rothe hai:
Ke jungle mein Sher khatre
mein hai?

Jamia Attack

“

*Innocent
Peacekeeper's men
mistook the library
for their training
ground.*

Godse Reborn

66

Godse is an oxymoron.
It's actually Devilse.

Judgment Day

"

Fascist Hindutva terror unmasked: Is this the Armageddon of Indian Democracy?

True Spirituality

"

Faith is meant to terrorize the Devil within. Not fellow humans.

Dissent and Democracy

"

*When Dissent
is awarded Life
Imprisonment under
the world's largest
democracy, it shows
even Hope is bleeding
in the claws of
Despair.*

Holocaust

"

*That Holocaust
happened under an
elected tyrant in
Germany is a wake-up
call for Indian Minorities. Muslims
AND Christians
included.*

Religiosity

"

*India is on the verge of a
catastrophic implosion
if the megawatt of
Religiosity goes unpurged.*

Mantra of Extremists

"

'Lynch pe milte hai'
The new mantra of
Indian right-wing
extremists.

About Author

Mujeeb Jaihoon, a prominent Indian author, is celebrated for his exploration of mystic and contemporary themes. His writing transcends language barriers, finding audiences across the globe through translations into French, Italian, Urdu, Tamil, and Malayalam. His insightful narratives have garnered admiration not only from literary enthusiasts but also from world statesmen and thought leaders. To delve deeper into Jaihoon's world, visit his website at **www.jaihoon.com** and connect with him on social media: @mujeebjaihoon